CW00321703

DESIGN
and decorate
KITCHENS

NEW HOLLAND

Lesley Taylor

To Ffion, my new baby daughter

First published in 1998 by
New Holland Publishers (UK) Ltd
London • Cape Town • Sydney • Auckland

24 Nutford Place
London W1H 6DQ
United Kingdom

80 McKenzie Street
Cape Town 8001
South Africa

Level 1, Unit 4, 14 Aquatic Drive
Frenchs Forest, NSW 2086
Australia

Unit 1A, 218 Lake Road
Northcote, Auckland
New Zealand

10 9 8 7 6 5 4 3 2

Copyright © 1998 in text Lesley Taylor
Copyright © 1998 in photographs New Holland Publishers (UK) Ltd
except those listed on page 79
Copyright © 1998 in artwork New Holland Publishers (UK) Ltd
Copyright © 1998 New Holland Publishers (UK) Ltd

All rights reserved. No part of this publication may be reproduced, stored in a
retrieval system, or transmitted in any form or by any means, electronic, mechanical,
photocopying, recording or otherwise, without the prior written permission of the
publishers and copyright holders.

ISBN 1 85368 934 3 (hbk)
ISBN 1 85368 946 7 (pbk)

Managing Editor: Coral Walker
Special photography: Janine Hosegood
Designed by: Grahame Dudley Associates
Editor: Emma Callery

Reproduction by Modern Age Repro House Ltd, Hong Kong
Printed and bound in Singapore by Tien Wah Press (Pte) Ltd

Contents

Introduction

I have been involved with many kitchen designs during my career, but it seems rather appropriate that while I was writing this book I was re-planning and extending the kitchen in my own home. Although many of you may think that it must be very easy for interior designers to design for their own house, I can assure you, when you have too much information it can be more difficult to make the decisions needed. Planning my kitchen, then, has given me an insight into how it feels when asked to make the choices that will affect your home. I hope this is reflected in the way the book has been written, giving you information in a very practical and helpful manner, with a few personal experiences added for good measure.

Design and Decorate Kitchens has been written to give you an insight into the world of kitchen design, explaining the styles now available and showing how they can be adapted to best suit your family and home. Conceptualizing – the planning and layout of your kitchen – is examined, giving you the knowledge and confidence to design your own kitchen or to understand and converse intelligently with any kitchen designer you choose to work with. The Focus File section on pages 60-77 then looks at the elements needed to complete a kitchen. Wallcoverings, flooring, worktops and lighting are all looked at in detail, ensuring you have all the information to make educated decisions that will avoid costly mistakes. My advice is to take your time and enjoy creating this all-important part of your home.

Layout *and* planning

GOOD DESIGN
▲ The positioning of the main appliances in the kitchen is very important. The cooker, refrigerator and sink should all be readily accessible and within an acceptable distance of each other.

ROOM TO WORK
▶ This chic modern kitchen offers ample work surfaces around the main food preparation area, something that is very important in a well-planned kitchen.

Good layout and planning are the keys to a successful kitchen. Decorative styles and aesthetic considerations are, of course, important. But the time spent on planning the room can make the difference between a nicely decorated kitchen and one that is not only decoratively pleasing but also functional, comfortable and 'user-friendly'.

The best layout for your kitchen very much depends on the individual needs of your particular family, so invest time in making a list of the facilities that your finished kitchen must offer to fulfil your requirements successfully. Some of the questions you may wish to consider are: Is your kitchen purely for the preparation and storage of food? Will you need to incorporate laundry facilities into the design? Do you need to include a dining area, and if so, is it purely for family eating or will you also use the space for entertaining guests? Will the space be used as a home study or for your children to do homework? Do you want the room to be multifunctional, with space for a television and seating area? Will it be the main room in the home that is used throughout the day for both food preparation, working and child minding?

Once you have established the main functions of your new kitchen, you can consider your personal preferences as to the finished look and atmosphere of the room, the style of appliances and the amount of storage you would like.

DIVIDED UP
◀ A beautifully crafted storage unit acts as a visual divide between the dining and cooking areas in this character cottage kitchen.

Certain styles of kitchens lend themselves to particular situations. Modern kitchens have easy-to-clean surfaces and incorporate the best storage options, making them ideal for a growing family. The country or cottage kitchen, on the other hand, may not offer the same variety of storage, but it does create a very relaxed atmosphere – ideal for those who enjoy a more laid-back lifestyle. Whatever style of kitchen appeals to you, consider the options available within that genre, and spend time deciding which one will best fit the requirements that you have listed for your ideal kitchen.

Once your preferences are clear in your mind you must then decide if you feel confident enough to plan your own kitchen or whether you would rather leave the layout and planning to an

CAREFUL PLANNING

▲ Narrow galley kitchens need careful planning to maximise the space. Here is a tried and tested layout with ample work-surfaces and all the facilities close to hand.

expert in kitchen design. Kitchen designers will visit your home to discuss your requirements, gaining enough information to produce a plan and layout that they feel will best meet your individual needs from within their range of products. Don't be afraid to shop around, and if you find a style of kitchen from one company that particularly appeals to you, but prefer the ideas on layout suggested by another, feel free to discuss these alternatives with the designer.

If you wish to plan the kitchen yourself, first make a scale drawing on paper. You will be amazed how different your room

will appear on a flat piece of paper, and how alternative layouts will become more apparent as you rearrange the elements on your plan.

Choose a convenient scale such as 1:20. This means that each centimetre (inch) on the plan represents 20 cm (20 in) in your kitchen. Measure the room using a metal tape measure and draw the plan onto graph paper. Include any permanent fixtures and fittings, such as doors, radiators and windows. Then, using the same scale, draw out the proportions of your preferred units and appliances, cut these out and name or number them for ease of identification. You can then explore the layout options available to you.

Consideration must be given to the plumbing and electrical facilities within the room, but don't be restricted by what is already installed. The simple relocation of a sink unit, for example, can have a great effect on the finished layout. Traditionally, many kitchen designers placed the sink in front of a window, presumably to give the person doing all the washing-up and laundry an interesting outlook. But as many kitchens now have washing machines and dishwashers, thankfully, considerably less time is spent on tasks by the sink. You may decide to use this area to position a dining table or breakfast bar, giving diners a brighter outlook.

Finally, don't be fooled by the idea that more is better: in a well-designed kitchen, the quality of the layout can far outweigh the quantity of units.

ULTRA CHIC
▲ Cooking appliances are the key components of any kitchen. In a modern environment you will want stream-lined units with a minimum of fuss. This ultra-chic stainless steel griddle is based on a Japanese design and cooks food swiftly without additional fat.

WICKER WORK
▼ Wicker baskets are very fashionable and they provide an excellent storage option for fresh produce, allowing air to circulate.

STYLE *file*

In many houses the kitchen is considered the centre of the home, a room in which the daily meals are prepared, the family gather to talk and eat, and a space where children can play and do their homework. So ample consideration must be given to planning and design, to ensure your kitchen can successfully fulfil the requirements of all the family.

A large percentage of accidents in the home occur in the kitchen, so when choosing fixtures, think about both their aesthetic qualities and their safety. Certain types of flooring, like highly-polished marble, for example, can look simply stunning in a modern kitchen. But if such a floor gets wet it can be a very dangerous surface. If yours is a busy family kitchen, it will have to withstand more wear and tear than that of a retired couple, say, so surfaces should be both hard wearing and easy to clean. Keep this uppermost in your mind when designing your kitchen as some products are more appropriate than others, depending on your circumstances. The cottage style, for example, may contain rustic pine or oak furniture and terracotta, slate or stone flooring, and while these combine to create a very welcoming atmosphere – ideal for a family – they also require more maintenance than a contemporary look with its easily cleaned units and hygienic ceramic or vinyl floors.

When selecting your kitchen, consider how the elements combine to create a look that will complement the style of your home and offer a practical and safe solution for your needs.

TOP LEFT
The old and the new in a winning combination. Traditional materials, such as granite and wood, team with stainless steel and modern paint effects.

BOTTOM LEFT
Freestanding units and a mixture of painted furniture make this country house-style kitchen warm and inviting – a place to dine as well as to cook.

TOP RIGHT
A well-designed small kitchen using laminated units and practical stainless steel. A wooden bar area fits snugly on one wall to create eating space.

BOTTOM RIGHT
The warmth of beech wood combined with cool chrome gives a relaxed, yet modern look. Spot-lighting draws the eye to a pair of uniquely patterned wall unit doors.

Traditional style

Traditional kitchens are those decorated with elements or themes derived from the past, but today many leading kitchen designers are mixing old themes with contemporary elements. The results are kitchens that work equally well in both traditional and modern homes. As with all good design, the best decorated rooms need not be totally pure in style. In fact, a blend of complementary elements, such as materials made from wood and stone combined with panelling and carvings, creates a very individual room.

If you wish to create a traditionally decorated room, then the items with the greatest influence on the finished look must be truly traditional. Individuality can then be achieved with the addition of smaller items in different styles.

CLEAR-CUT LINES

▶ This kitchen is simple yet practical, offering ample storage in an individual style. The cupboard doors have been made from tongue and groove and painted in neutral tones for a classic feel. Traditional door furniture – hinges and handles – in black iron give an authentic, old-fashioned touch.

PINE AND TERRACOTTA

▲ Antique pine lends a mellow warmth to any kitchen and this stylish room combines the beauty of natural wood and terracotta. Integrated modern appliances such as refrigerators and dish-washers can be concealed within the run of units, keeping the lines of the kitchen as simple and traditional as possible.

OLD AND NEW

◄ Traditional elements, such as the Belfast or butler's sink, are enjoying a revival, and combine well with a built-in cooker and hob.

Clever colour accents
in a traditional

I have a particular love of what are best called 'personally styled' rooms. These are rooms that have been decorated to create a look which does not fall into a particular style or period but simply portrays the designer's or client's personality and individual taste.

Occasionally, a leading designer will create a particular look that then starts a trend. It is very difficult to analyse what makes this type of room successful, as by its very nature it does not fall into any one category. Sometimes there is no specific reason for the individual elements combining to create a pleasing room – they just do.

The room featured here is just such an example. Traditional rustic pine has been combined with Victorian-style painted furniture to create a unique kitchen. The strongest elements in the kitchen are the crimson-painted base and wall units in the centre of the far wall; the additional units look almost incidental by their side. The mock dresser, made especially striking by using a brilliant brick red paint, is the focal point of the room, as it would be in a more conventional kitchen. The continuous wooden work-tops also link the various coloured base units effectively to create a sense of unity.

The result is a totally fitted kitchen, but because

THE BEAUTY OF WOOD
◄ Mix painted and natural wood to create the look achieved here. Combine old and new timbers – waxing, staining or varnishing them as you wish and teaming them with freshly painted surfaces. Use an eggshell, gloss or satin oil-based paint for a durable finish.

wooden kitchen

of the variations in colours and textures, it has the eclectic atmosphere of an unfitted one. It is a good example of a kitchen that combines the old and the new in an understated way.

This type of kitchen would work especially well in a country cottage where the occupier feels comfortable with all styles of traditional furniture. It would look equally good in a town house if the occupant has a love for country simplicity and is looking for a style that blends in with the architecture of a period home.

COLOUR THEORY

▲ Consider the effect that colour can have on the balance of the finished room. A knowledge of colour theory can be very helpful here as the use of certain colours could make a room appear longer or wider. In general, warm colours advance and cool colours recede.

Soft shades revive
an old kitchen

A few years ago, kitchen designers looked for inspiration to the traditional cook's kitchen found in the servants' quarters of large, old houses. This led to a revival of the painted wooden kitchen. The old kitchens were very well designed with ample storage, and incorporated whole walls of cupboards and drawers. The up-to-date version of this area offers the home a well-organized space with a traditional air. The cream paintwork associated with this style of kitchen is still very popular, but has also given way to a more contemporary range of colours, giving the basic design a modern feel.

The kitchen featured here is the perfect example of a new style of cook's kitchen where modern paints are mixed with traditional pieces of furniture to create a warm and welcoming family space. The beauty of this sort of kitchen is its ability to work well in so many different types of house. It looks equally at home in a small, surburban house as it does in a large old country manor.

Appliances such as dishwashers are housed in matching units to help retain the character of this kind of kitchen. While most styles of hob and oven would work successfully in this setting, traditional ranges, like the one featured opposite, fully enhance the design features that were originally part of this type of kitchen.

INDIVIDUAL CERAMICS

▶ Ceramic tiles have a rich and interesting history. Originating in Persia and China, it was many hundreds of years before glazed tiles were discovered in Europe. Today, many manufacturers and some individual potteries offer handmade tiles fashioned by traditional methods.

This particular colour scheme uses light yellow painted walls as a summery backdrop behind the peppermint green units and painted furniture. Schemes featuring traditional wallpapers or stencilling would be equally successful. If you choose this option, ensure the wallpapers used are vinyl coated to withstand the moisture created by cooking. Likewise, use paints that are specifically designed for steamy kitchen use. These are usually water based and incredibly easy to use. The tiled walls behind the work surfaces and cooking area are a practical – as well as decorative – finishing touch as they are quick to put up and easy to wipe down.

CHANGING THE COLOURS

▲ Painted kitchens always offer the option of re-styling as you can simply change the colour in years to come. This means you can give your room a new lease of life without installing a new kitchen. Simply sand back the original woodwork to enable the new paint to key, and apply at least two coats of suitable paint.

Old-fashioned charm from
traditional materials

This beautiful, sunlit kitchen includes all the elements associated with traditional styling: stone, wicker, mellow golden timber and painted walls. Yet because of the style of the wooden kitchen units it has a refreshingly modern feel. While other elements of this room are very rustic in character, these modern-shaped units look completely at home because they are made from natural timber. In fact, natural timber acts very well as a bridge between two distinctive styles. The same basic shape manufactured in a different material would look completely out of place in this setting.

The room has a wonderful feeling of spaciousness, due to the plentiful natural light. This is also enhanced by the lack of wall units. Instead, an open-style plate rack offers additional storage without completely dominating the wall area.

This kitchen offers the best of both worlds, the relaxed atmosphere associated with a traditional setting but the practical advantages that come from modern styling. Items like the Belfast sink and the granite work surfaces have been chosen not only because of their association with the traditional kitchen but because they are so practical. Likewise, the wicker baskets form ideal storage containers for fresh produce as they allow air to circulate freely.

The basic colour scheme of this room falls into the natural or neutral category. This group of colours ranges from browns and creams through to whites, and appear on a regular basis with

NATURAL SURFACES
▲ In place of a granite worktop consider marble or ceramic tiles, each of which is hard-wearing, easy to clean and available in a great range of colours and styles.

and greenery

each new trend, mainly because they are so easy to live with. While this type of colour scheme is often full of texture and warmth, it can look bland unless there is plenty of tonal variety in the room. This means adjusting the depths of colour to add interest and dimension to the basic scheme. Imagine this room as a black and white picture and you will see what is meant by tonal variety. Even the stencilled border offers a change in tone. Another tip to pep up a neutral scheme is to add an 'accent' colour. Here, the plants offer the perfect solution, providing a much-needed splash of green to the room.

SUNLIT KITCHEN

◀ In this warm and sunny kitchen, stone tiling provides a cool and practical floor covering. Although an expensive option, stone floors are extremely durable and can be softened with a rug or natural matting.

Sage and ivory
team in a practical

CONCEALED STORAGE

▲ A 'food centre' with refrigerator and microwave oven is cleverly concealed behind mock façades.

SIMPLE CHANGES

▼ One of the simplest ways to change the style of a kitchen is to replace the knobs and handles. Try specialist door furniture suppliers for a really wide range.

The kitchen is undoubtedly one of the most expensive rooms in the home to decorate, and that is why many people look for one that will not go out of fashion very quickly. This is another reason for the popularity of the traditional kitchen, as these have become classic designs that have successfully passed the test of time.

The kitchen featured here relies on excellent craftsmanship and good traditional design to give the room its distinctive, age-less quality. This does not mean, however, that the units are reproductions of an original painted kitchen cupboards. In fact, there are a number of design details incorporated by the designer to make this cook's kitchen very much a room for today. Not only are the best working appliances and cooking facilities supplied, but there are certain elements that have been exaggerated in proportion to add an interesting twist to the overall look of the finished room. The substantial curved cornices, for example, are a refreshing change from the normal mitred corner detail that is normally associated with this style of fitting. The drawer knobs, too, are larger than you would expect to find on surfaces of this size. The overall effect of these details is stylish, practical and full of individuality.

Colour also plays a big part in the design of this kitchen. Sage green has been chosen as the primary colour, with cream to add relief and natural tones for contrast. The base units provide the main block of colour with a dash of cream added via the door knobs. The Corian worktop is also

cook's kitchen

cream, keeping the overall look very crisp and fresh. Above this begins a full height run of Delft-influenced ceramic tiles, again in sage and cream. These create a soft background pattern while providing a practical and easy-to-clean wall cladding. Note how a moulding tile has been positioned at picture rail height to add a traditional detail to the room.

The cream wall units are mounted in front of this patterned backdrop. The designer has chosen to use this pale colour to keep the look as airy as possible. This is most important where the run of units is confined mainly to one wall. If the wall units had been in sage, the balance of the room would have been lost.

DARK AND LIGHT
▲ Sage and cream are combined in perfect balance to create a traditional kitchen with a modern slant.

Contemporary style

STREAMLINED
▲ Bright blocks of colour and straight runs of units make this kitchen truly contemporary.

Every few years there is a trend in interior design which, as with fashion, filters from the leading designers through to the high street. Over the last two decades we have seen a Victorian revival and the return of the country interior. But this has now made way for a new and refreshing trend that incorporates the bright and confident use of colour and clean, simple lines. It is the return of the streamlined and hi-tech contemporary interior.

The word 'contemporary' is described in the dictionary as being of the same age or era, which simply means this style is current or of this period. So by its very nature, contemporary design includes a number of up-to-date styles, including the clean, modern look that is now so popular. Choosing to decorate your kitchen in a contemporary way gives you a wide design spectrum to work within, along with the opportunity of being creative and individual.

If you are planning a contemporary kitchen, you may wish to

CHERRY WOOD AND BLACK PAINT
▶ One contemporary kitchen designer celebrates the style of the innovative and highly original Scottish designer and architect, Charles Rennie Mackintosh, with his interpretation of a 'Mackintosh' kitchen.

choose blocks of bright, plain colours incorporated into highly glossed kitchen units, or modular wooden furniture teamed with chrome and modern plastics. Whatever you choose, this style enables you to use bold colour with confidence.

INDUSTRIAL STYLE

▲ Many contemporary schemes include industrial-looking elements. This one includes chrome, glass and strong ochre-coloured rendered walls. Notice, too, the smooth-flowing, wavy lines of the vivid blue laminated kitchen units.

CHROME AND GLASS

◀ Free-standing modular units are readily available from a number of chain stores. They offer unlimited storage options in the modern home, particularly in a kitchen where attractive, but practical, shelf-space is at a premium.

Natural textures and
neutral tones create

This stunning kitchen gives natural products like timber and slate a slick, modern look. The designer has harnessed all the beauty of natural wood, making its colour variation and graining an important part of the kitchen design. This results in a mellow room with the wood's natural character adding design detail, as opposed to fussy panelling and mouldings, for interest.

The mixing of textures within a room can add as much interest as the cleverest blending of patterns. Here, green-grey slate offers the room a very practical floor covering that

GRID LINES

▼ The elements of this kitchen make great play of squares and rectangles in its storage, flooring and the glass partition. The overall effect is one of simplicity and modernity.

chic, modern style

contrasts beautifully with the mellow, smooth texture of the wooden furniture. It also sits very comfortably alongside the simple white walls and fresh, cool qualities of the glass blockwork partition. All of these products have been chosen to add variation of texture, and therefore visual enhancement, to the room. The colour palette is limited to neutral tones with shades of muted green on the marble work surfaces, cushion covers and checkered slate floor.

Note how the far wall is fully fitted with elegant and stream-lined units from floor to ceiling. They keep the lines of the kitchen as simple as possible and also raise the ceiling height in the room. Indeed, simplicity is the key to this room's success and each element relies on its natural beauty to add detail to the room. There are no curtains, and no additional patterns to detract from the character brought by each individual, carefully chosen item.

This is a kitchen designed for entertaining in style – there is ample storage for drinks, the glasses are within easy reach and the work tops have been specially designed to incorporate a wooden chopping block into the practical and easy-to-clean slate slabs. Chrome appliances and accessories are not just practical and smart – they help to enhance the modern feel of a kitchen. Each of these small details ensures that both entertaining and food preparation are as enjoyable as possible.

MODERN-DAY DISPLAY

◀ The concept of the traditional dresser to display kitchenware is still popular. Today, glass-fronted cupboards serve the same purpose and help to break up a run of wall units.

STREAMLINED HEATING

▼ Keep the lines simple – contemporary heating comes in the form of wall-mounted radiator panels, available in a wide colour range.

Refreshing pastels
transform a small area

Most of us are now aware of the benefits of a kitchen/diner – a room in which to relax and entertain as well as to prepare and eat our meals. Some people will relocate their kitchen to a larger room in the home, such as a rarely used formal dining room. If this is not the answer for you, then a single-storey extension on an existing room, or a conservatory housing the working kitchen, may be the perfect solution. The pastel-painted kitchen featured here is an excellent example of a well-designed and compact kitchen positioned in a single-storey extension to the side of a living space.

COLOUR CONFIDENCE

▼ It is the confident use of colour which lifts this kitchen from the mundane to the fabulous. The choice and balance of colours – pale mauve teamed with the palest creamy lemon and cobalt blue – can be carried from the overall decor through to the smaller details.

When planning a kitchen extension or refurbishment, it is a good idea to decide how much of your time will be spent preparing meals in the room, and how much time will be taken with activities more associated with a living or sitting room. If your kitchen is well designed, a great deal can be achieved in a very limited space: good planning is the key to a successful working kitchen (see pages 6-9). As much can be achieved by an organized cook in a small kitchen as in the most generous of spaces. You may therefore be surprised at how little space you need to allocate to the working kitchen. Really, all that is needed is adequate storage, a cooker, refrigerator, sink and sufficient preparation and serving spaces.

The attractive kitchen featured here benefits from the additional natural light supplied by

the sky lights and further enhanced by the chosen colour scheme. Lemon-green wall and base units sit very happily on a lavender blue background. It is interesting to note that pastels are the only colours on the colour wheel that you can guarantee will never clash; it doesn't matter what combination you team together, they will always work successfully. The lavender blue walls and ceiling also act to maximize the available space as all blue-based, cool colours appear to recede, and therefore create the impression of pushing back the walls that they decorate. Tonal interest is provided by the dark blue stained glass in the windows and the inset border on the tiled splashback. This important detail acts to emphasize the area, adding depth to a basically pastel colour scheme.

LAVENDER ISLAND

▲ The island unit provides an additional work surface and lots of storage; it also acts as a natural divide between the working area of the kitchen and the dining or sitting room.

White and chrome
mellowed with

As with all colour schemes, the lighter the colours used, the larger the area in which they appear will look. Here, a fairly narrow kitchen leading to a dining area has benefited from the use of pure white units. Look at the area where the kitchen meets the dining room and imagine how tall and narrow the opening would have seemed if the units on either side had been a deeper colour.

White can have the disadvantage of giving a room a clinical and sometimes cold appearance, especially in north-facing rooms. This is because blocks of white can appear grey when natural light lacks the sun's warmth. One way to add softness to a white room is to opt for white or cream with a lemon base. There are, however, other ways of adding warmth to a basically white colour scheme. Using a warm colour like peach or terracotta in tiling, flooring or furnishings, for example, would soften the room, but beware, as a large expanse of white with a minimal amount of these colours can look contrived and quite uneasy on the eye.

One of the most successful ways of bringing a mellow warmth to a white room is to use natural timber, which has a way of softening the hard edges of a colour scheme. In this kitchen, the timber flooring, in particular, adds a casualness to a room that would have looked cold and unwelcoming if clad in more obvious white, grey or black ceramic or marble tiles.

LIGHTLY TOASTED
▼ The traditional toaster – with its enduring sense of style – has made a comeback and is the perfect design feature in a chrome kitchen.

warm timber

The pattern in which the timber floor has been laid also has an effect on the appearance of the finished room. If the timber strips had been set to run the length of the kitchen through to the dining area, the floor would have looked longer, and the kitchen even narrower. If the strips had run horizontally, the room would have benefited from the appearance of extra width, but the lines of the kitchen might have appeared hard and square. The perfect solution was to run them diagonally, adding width and softer lines to the room.

COOL CHROME
▼ This kitchen looks extremely smart with its chrome appliances and accessories. Chrome has long been used in commercial settings because of its practical and hygienic qualities, and these have now been harnessed by designers to add a functional feel to domestic kitchens.

Clever colour
combinations work

▲ Broken colour effects are popular decorative techniques which recently have been revived. The method creates 'moving colour' and in the kitchen these effects provide a scintillating scheme.

STRIKING BLIND
▶ Many kitchens forego curtains in favour of more practical blinds. In a daring colour scheme such as this, opt for a striking blind to pull all the colour elements together.

This kitchen is an excellent example of the new trend in interiors. It demonstrates a new-found confidence in the application of colour and shows the ability of contemporary designers to blend a variety of textures and finishes successfully. A knowledge of the colour wheel and colour theory is invaluable here, as harnessing the power of colour is integral to the success of this – some would say – daringly finished room.

Emerald green fitted units – the central feature of this colour scheme – nestle among a variety of colours, all of which contain a certain amount of red. Terracotta, pink and lavender are harmonious colours which sit to one side of the colour wheel, and therefore naturally work well together when used in certain proportions. They also enhance the colours that they lie opposite, one of which is green, thereby explaining why these colours work together so successfully.

Many people find the bold use of colour in this style of contemporary setting harsh. But the colourwashed finish on most of the painted walls in this room adds softness to the colour scheme. This paint effect also acts as a textural link to the pale terracotta flooring, which might have appeared out of place if the room had been decorated using the same colours in their denser, more natural form.

To achieve this bold style of colourwashing, paint the wall surface with a pale-coloured base

in harmony

coat and leave it to dry. Then water down your chosen decorative colour (emulsion paint is the most straightforward). Use 1 part paint to 5 parts water. Working on one wall at a time, apply the paint with a 5 cm (2 in) wide brush, moving the brush quickly in all directions. Occasionally stir the diluted paint mixture as the water and emulsion will begin to separate. As the paint dries, 'paint' over the surface again, but without actually loading any more paint onto the brush. This will soften the initial paint marks.

LIGHT EFFECTS
▲ To make the best of a medley of colours you need to get the lighting just right. In the absence of natural light, use pure white halogen lighting, adding interest with spots and concealed lights.

Clever layout creates
a modern kitchen diner

Large rooms like this one can be very effectively split into defined areas because of their generous proportions. It is not merely acceptable to use such a treatment in a large room, it is positively beneficial as the overall effect can often be better when furniture is not just placed around the edges. This invariably leaves a large void in the centre of the room, which can really only be filled with a dining table and chairs. Here, however, the units have been positioned to create a partition between the cooking area and the dining space. The units in this run have varying heights to ensure the dining area remains integral to the main room while still offering maximum storage and working space. Because the partition runs from one wall and down through the centre of the room, all services like electricity and water can be run from the outside wall and through the base units. If these units had been positioned as a central divider, with equal space for access on both sides, these essential services would have had to be run under the floor, or a step up onto a false floor.

COLOUR COMBO

▼ This kitchen uses a great combination of easy-on-the-eye colours – off-white, green and honey brown.

The same principle applies to the 'island' or central cooking unit, which does require a source of electricity to run under the floor. Always remember to account for supplies of water and power when planning the kitchen. If you are uncertain, seek the advice of a kitchen fitter who will tell you what is practical, feasible and within your budget.

The splendid central unit has a generous work space, which doubles as an additional, informal eating area.

The room has a very mellow, yet contemporary feel to it. Off-white worktops team with natural alder wood in a gently curving design. A green contrast is incorporated in the side units on the main run and in the pattern on the ceramic floor. These colours continue through to the dining area, where a golden, natural floor matting further enhances the division of space within the room. Finally, the room is well-coordinated using a mixture of natural wood, warm terracotta and an array of fresh green foliage. These final elements soften what could have been a rather clinical look and provide a pleasant aspect to a modern room.

TWO FROM ONE
▲ This smooth working kitchen is the essence of good design, where space has been maximized and two rooms have been created from one.

Cottage kitchens

To the traditionalists among us, the word 'cottage' conjures up images of rustic timber, time-worn stone, quarry floors, and back-to-basics furnishings and fittings. To the more adventurous, however, the idea of the cottage interior offers the opportunity of creating a room with traditional cottage features mixed with more contemporary elements, complementary to a rural setting.

COUNTRY HALLMARKS
▲ Antique pine and moss green woodwork are hallmarks of the country kitchen. The old-fashioned stoneware, the range and marble-topped butcher's block contribute to the look.

Regardless of their individual elements, cottage kitchens have a welcoming, unpretentious air. This is perpetuated by natural products and home-spun fabrics. The last few years have seen a surge in the popularity of distressed painted furniture, and rustic flooring; even modern paint finishes now emulate aged plaster walls. These contemporary elements are successfully used in the most modern of rooms. But because of their origins, they also work very well in a cottage environment. So it comes as no surprise to find a new wave of interiors incorporating these interpretations of traditional items.

The one thing they all have in common is their natural properties. Wrought iron is the perfect example: this is a traditional product and would have featured in the cottage kitchen in forged door furniture and the cooking range. Nowadays it can be seen as contemporary dining furniture and accessories. Likewise, there has been a resurgence in natural paints such as distemper and limewash, which bring greater authenticity to today's cottage kitchen.

PAINT EFFECTS

▼ Contemporary elements like modern paint techniques and painted furniture in modern colours sit perfectly in this cottage kitchen. The overwhelming feeling is one of traditional quality and natural rustic charm.

OLD BEAMS

◀ Exposed beams make an architectural statement in a cottage kitchen. New 'fake' beams can give the illusion of a traditional form of construction inside the most modern properties.

Old-fashioned kitchenware *provides a*

Pine is one of the timbers most often associated with the cottage interior, and there is still a large choice of pine furniture available, the majority of which is reproduction. With the revival of interest in pine furniture over the past decade or so, most of the original pieces were quickly snapped up. Fortunately, there are now a number of manufacturers using traditional methods to produce excellent pieces of furniture from reclaimed timber. These make a perfectly acceptable substitute, while having the benefit of being available to order in any shape and size imaginable. This makes the job of creating a practical and authentic-looking cottage kitchen ever simpler.

Originally, only free-standing pieces of furniture would have been found in the cottage kitchen, but nowadays a careful blend of both fitted and unfitted pieces can fulfil the needs of the modern family without straying too far from a traditional style of decor. The back-to-basics feel of a traditional cottage can also be retained by concealing modern appliances behind the unit fronts.

The cooking range is a dominant feature in the traditional cottage kitchen. There are now a number of 'traditional'-style cookers available, inspired by the popularity of solid fuel and gas-powered enamelled ranges. Originally, the range was both a reliable cooking appliance and a source of heat for the home. The new wave of gas and electric cookers, however, are purely a cooking facility. The positioning of the traditional enamelled range was restricted because it needed to be vented-

FINISHING TOUCHES
▼ Old-fashioned enamelled tinware and china can be bought quite inexpensively to complete the country look.

homely look

NOSTALGIC ACCESSORIES

◄ Traditional accessories and clutter are all part of the character associated with a cottage-style kitchen. No matter how confined the space – and country kitchens by their very nature are small – be sure to have a goodly mix of china, enamelled tinware and nostalgic paraphernalia.

CHECK OUT

▼ Check fabrics have long been associated with country-style decor. Use them to make simple curtains and pelmets for the window, or to cover unsightly areas that lurk below the sink.

it would have been placed close to an outside wall. Today, power flues can be used to draw the fumes a greater distance, giving modern kitchen designers more flexibility when planning.

The kitchen featured here not only uses traditional materials, like pine, and products such as the cooking range and the Belfast sink, but it also uses traditional colours to evoke the nostalgia of an old-fashioned cottage kitchen. Buttermilk walls give the room a warmth reminiscent of age-stained paintwork, while deep bottle green adds depth and definition to the colour scheme.

Fitted kitchen given a
country touch with fabric

As with all interior design styles there are many interpretations of an original look. These normally incorporate up-to-date features and products designed to make maintenance as simple as possible, enabling the room to include the best of modern design within a traditional atmosphere.

The kitchen featured here is manufactured from solid oak, a material traditionally associated with the country kitchen. The decorator has decided to enhance its traditional qualities further by covering the kitchen walls with a pretty floral stripe wallpaper, setting the table with a patchwork-printed fabric as a

TRADITIONAL DETAILING

▼ The traditional cottage kitchen features free-standing items of furniture, which do not always fulfil the needs of the modern family. A modern kitchen incorporating traditional details and dressed with cottage-style furnishings may be the perfect solution.

and flowers

contrast and dressing the windows with check curtains. The same checked fabric has been used for the frilled and deep-buttoned seat cushions tied with generous bows to the back of each chair. These, together with the accessories and details like the dried flowers displayed above the wall units, create a modern kitchen with a distinctly rural feel.

This cottage kitchen is fully fitted and therefore offers ample storage within concealed appliances, features which give the family a practical working environment. A deep drawer next to the oven is an excellent feature that is now incorporated into many kitchens as pots and pans can be stacked and retrieved more easily from here than from the back of a cupboard.

The worktops are clad in ceramic tiles that continue up the wall, creating a hygienic, easily cleaned surface. Care must be taken, however, if using ceramics on worktop surfaces as some glazes may be susceptible to staining. Also, always use the correct adhesives and grouts to ensure an impervious joint where no bacteria can grow.

The floor tiles provide an interesting variation on the cottage hearth rug. To be practical – as this is a family room – a checkerboard pattern has been created in the centre of the floor. This has the effect of breaking up what could otherwise be a large expanse of cream tiles. It also makes the dining area look more homely. The choice of colours links in with the work surface tiles and checked curtains, and the cream wallpaper.

FINISHING TOUCH
▲ Swags of dried flowers are the perfect country accessory for a kitchen such as this.

SOFT FURNISHINGS
▼ Look in any fabric store and you will find a wide variety of checked and floral fabrics from which you can make cushion covers, table-cloths and curtains for a country-style kitchen.

Rustic brick and timber -
the ultimate

**BRICK
CLADDING**

▲ Rustic brick and traditional blue and white china are key elements in the country-style kitchen. If you are unable to expose natural brickwork, modern brick cladding is actually a very realistic alternative.

Nearly two decades ago, a leading kitchen design house introduced their simple country, hand-made pine kitchen and it took the industry by storm. Its continued popularity has made this style of kitchen a design classic. Traditional panelled doors, pine knobs and fretwork are all important features of this style of country kitchen. Other features that recall the simple cottage style are the plate drainage racks above the sink area, small drawers for storing all those bits and pieces that always seem to amass in the kitchen, and cupboard doors with glass panels.

Rustic timbers feature heavily in the design of this kitchen, both as beams on the ceiling and as supporting upright posts, giving the kitchen an authentic appearance. If your kitchen is not of this period, introducing fake timbers can set the scene.

A flagstone floor is both practical and beautiful, and in this case it blends with the exposed rustic brickwork. There is a wide range of flooring tiles available and if you can't run to the expense of original stone tiles, cushioned flooring is a good imitation – and it is warmer underfoot, too. If you want to use brick in your kitchen, as here, a secondhand brick is the best for this setting as its mellow tones complement the woodwork and the slightly crumbled edges have a worn softness not found in modern bricks.

Above the preparation area an old-fashioned rack – often used for airing clothes – holds saucepans and cookware. It is both practical and a charming decorative feature.

country kitchen

Finally, there is the traditional cooking range, housed in a brick arched recess, reminiscent of the inglenook fireplaces of years gone by. This traditional cooking appliance is the main feature of the kitchen, emphasizing the fact that the cottage kitchen represents the heart of the home, where the family gathers by the warmth of the range to be fed good, hearty, home-produced meals. Today's ranges are available in a far greater number of colours than in years gone by, making them traditional and yet also contemporary in their feel.

COPPER
▲ An authentic touch: antique copper saucepans hanging from the wall or an overhead rack. Buy reproduction pans if you can't get originals.

BARLEY TWIST
▼ The attractive scrolls running up each of the units draw together the disparate elements in this kitchen.

Family kitchens

In terms of decoration, family kitchens can fall into any design category, but at the planning stage, additional time and thought

must be given to ensuring that the family kitchen fulfils the needs of each person. Safety is of utmost importance, and the design should be practical, too, offering adequate storage, cooking and working facilities. The working area will often extend beyond the preparation of food, as this is quite likely the place where children play or study under a parent's watchful eye.

A ROOM TO ENJOY

▲ This splendid kitchen is clearly the hub of the family home. It is used for both social and practical purposes.

The best way to tackle the planning is to note the primary functions of the finished room. List them in priority order and the available space can then be allocated suitably, so you create a room specially tailored to the needs of your family.

When choosing products for the kitchen, select with care as the room will suffer more wear than that used by a retired couple, for example. It is important to strike a balance between the practical and the aesthetic, too. If you have a young family, there is a wide range of kitchen safety equipment available, covering everything from door locks for your cupboards to safety guards for the cooker. These are essential for a safe environment, and once the family has grown, they can all be removed. This means that the kitchen of your dreams can be a reality, even though you have a busy, growing family. Safety does not have to be at the expense of style – good planning can supply both.

GENEROUS PROPORTIONS

▲ This kitchen has a generous dining/ working area that is ideal for both family gatherings and the quieter moments when the children need time to concentrate and study within earshot of a parent.

GOOD PLANNING

◄ This galley kitchen may not offer a large dining or play area, but the space available has been used to produce an efficient kitchen equipped to service the needs of a growing family. Cooking, food storage and laundry requirements are all succinctly catered for.

Old-world charm
for relaxed

This authentic rural kitchen is undoubtedly unique in its origin, but its charm and simplicity would be easy to replicate for anyone eager to create a similar look in their home.

The flooring is traditional slate slabs, which have the advantage of being extremely hard wearing, although a little chilly underfoot. This type of flooring is now widely available, as are a number of variations on this theme. African slate slab, for example, has the same qualities as traditional slate, with the addition of a vibrant blend of rustic colour, while Venetian stone offers a soft, off-white floor with the same traditional feel.

NOSTALGIA
▼ Recreating a family room like this would not be difficult: it contains a carefree mix of inexpensive items acquired over the years.

family gatherings

The walls have been painted with a blue-tinted oil-based paint which is easy to wipe clean, is hard-wearing and gives a soft sheen to the walls. It is also of a type that adheres to both timber and plaster work, enabling the timber partition to be painted with the same product. This timber wall houses the stairs leading to the upper floor, and while in modern houses it would be constructed from either blocks and plaster or timber and plasterboard, the original timber planks are on display here adding to the atmosphere of the room. This could easily be copied using tongue and groove timber in the modern kitchen.

The generous cooking range is original, but due to its timeless efficiency, is of a type still manufactured today. There are also modern cookers available which are designed to look like the traditional range, but these are only for cooking, so you might prefer to have a modern range which can heat the water and the house, too.

While the cooker is undoubtedly the most important item in this kitchen, the dining table and chairs are the core around which life in the kitchen revolves. This table is served by six raffia ladder-back chairs and one pine carver. The mixture of two paint colours and natural timber adds to the relaxed atmosphere, a trick that can easily be copied.

THE RANGE

◄ Ranges like this are manufactured in a wider choice of colours than used to be the case. They are the perfect form of cooker for the family kitchen as they keep the room warm and cosy in the cold winter months.

FLOOR COVERINGS

▼ Oriental rugs need not be expensive; a great many passable imitations are made that would add colour and warmth to a kitchen that sports hard stone flooring.

Vivid colours
add vibrancy to

Most families need to find a great deal of space for the many time-saving devices now available, such as the microwave oven, food processor, the juicer, or even the doughnut maker. A fitted kitchen is the best solution for people who need generous amounts of storage unless, of course, the house has a traditional pantry space. One of the other benefits of fitted kitchens is that they are available in a wide range of styles and finishes, most of which have been designed and manufactured to offer the best in storage and are easy to clean and maintain. This kitchen offers all these benefits, with the addition of a bright, fun and safe environment for the whole family.

The oven is housed within a wall unit ensuring it is out of the reach of the children and also at a level which is easily accessible. Directly above the cooker there is a small microwave oven fitted in one of the cupboards, again out of the children's reach and hidden from view, keeping the kitchen as streamlined as possible. The hob is surrounded by a removable chrome safety guard – a vital safety device to prevent a curious toddler from pulling down a burning pot on his or her head. The controls to the hob are sited above rather than underneath. This clever positioning keeps the controls away from children's ever-inquisitive fingers but at a perfect height for an adult.

In a well-designed fitted kitchen such as this, all other appliances such as the refrigerator, freezer and dishwasher can be

soft background tones

FAMILY PLANNING

◀ This fitted kitchen in light beech and pale green has been specifically planned for a growing family, offering safety features and a streamlined, ergonomic layout to make it pleasant to work in while providing plenty of floor and tabletop space.

installed behind units, in the same way as the microwave. The kitchen remains neat and the appliances hidden.

Decoratively, the light green and pale beech units are the perfect simple backdrop to the brightly coloured accessories that have been chosen to enhance the room. When decorating any room that will regularly house children, do not forget to allow space for all their colourful toys and accessories.

BRIGHT LIGHTS

▼ Vivid colours in modern, translucent plastic or glass light up a primarily neutral kitchen.

A contemporary edge to
a traditional kitchen

Having the confidence to mix different styles purely because you like them is a wonderful attribute. It is normally only through trial and error that you can discover if contrasting ideas will work, and if you like them and can live with them in your home, it is the perfect opportunity to run with instinct.

Sometimes it is very difficult to analyse rooms where different looks have been used successfully together. For example, this mixture of contemporary black and cream furnishings with traditional pine, may only work well because of the balance that has been created in the room. The basic kitchen has been framed by modern wallpaper and a border, while the tablecloth echoes their colour and design, drawing them into the centre of the room.

A few days ago, a friend who is decorating her kitchen asked for my advice. She had chosen a dark oak traditional kitchen and was pondering on her next design decision as the units would fit in well with either one of two styles. Should she give the room a country atmosphere? This is a format that she favours and has lived with successfully for many years. Or should she take a more formal approach, making the room more like that in a town house? Her choice would determine whether the ceiling should be clad with timber beams or whether a decorative cove should be installed.

As she is very familiar with my own method of decorating, and was well aware of my love of rooms in which styles are blended, she felt that maybe she should gather enough confidence to use

both approaches in her room. In theory, this sounds a good compromise, but if you are adding architectural details, it is important they favour only one style so that the room remains intrinsically whole. In this case, rustic beams would look completely out of character with the room if an ornate coving were also to be used. My advice was to decide on which look she wanted to establish as the room's central theme, and then if she wanted to add some contrast, she could do this with the interior decor and accessories.

BALANCING ACT

▼ Combining traditional fitted units with contemporary decor can work well as long as the correct balance is made. Here, the wallpaper surrounds the kitchen and the eye is drawn into the centre by the boldly patterned tablecloth.

Country & town house

The country and town house styles of decorating fall somewhere between grand and rustic. Traditionally, many country house owners also had a house in the town, which is where the crossover of style originates. The owners were richer than their country cottage neighbours, so the furniture purchased for such houses was grander – yet subject to the decorative trends of the day – while still blending in perfectly with a country style of furnishing, such as full-blown rose chintz fabric.

PERIOD STYLE
▲ Reproduction antique French-style dining chairs grace the dining table in this kitchen. Note how well they blend with traditional practical elements like the plate rack and simple wall-mounted shelves.

The country house kitchen originally offered the occupant the best design that money could buy, but in a distinctly more casual style than in the town house. Many of the larger country houses had lavishly equipped kitchens with walls of built-in storage and generous range cookers.

This is where the traditional fitted kitchen originated, either in natural timber or painted, as in many turn-of-the-century houses. They were designed to be practical with hard-wearing stone or quarry tiled floors, and large pine or scrubbed oak tables. These are elements that can still be seen in the country house styled kitchen, but as these rooms are not purely for the use of food preparation, they may be blended with the somewhat grander kinds of furniture found in other rooms around the home.

TRADITIONAL PAINTS

▼ Painted traditional kitchen units have a more formal appearance than their pine or oak alternatives, ideal for reproducing this style of kitchen.

COUNTRY HOUSE DETAILS

◀ Traditional rural features like rustic flooring, pressed tiles and basketware are teamed with a smart painted kitchen to produce a more formal country house style.

Making the most of
light and space

What style of kitchen would you create if you blended hand-crafted traditional pine units, a smart terracotta and ceramic floor and a stunning conservatory? Well, you will have a unique room, that combines rustic charm with the elegance that comes from a large, traditional glass extension.

The expanses of glass make makes this room look quite light and airy. However, the kitchen does not lack privacy even though the generous sash window has no curtaining. Instead,

TILED FLOORING

▶ The terracotta and textured ceramic floor combines the rustic qualities associated with terracotta and quarry tiles with the easy maintenance of a glazed ceramic tile. It also adds a block of pattern to the large floor area, reducing its apparent size and making it seem less daunting.

PAINTED GLASS
▶ With a little practice it is straightforward to give your windows a stained glass effect with modern glass paints. They add a beautiful translucent colour and create privacy on lower panes of glass.

CUTLERY HOLDERS
▶ These pigeonholes are ideal for storing everyday knives, forks and spoons.

the lower two panes have been decorated with glass paints to obscure vision into the room. These paints are available at various craft outlets and by mail order. Although they require a little practice, the paints are not beyond the talents of most of us, and they are effective in providing privacy without cutting out too much light.

Attention to detail is very important in this room. Note the room divider, for example. It has been made from the same timber as the main kitchen units and makes a definite 'partition' between the main food preparation area and the dining space. The open shelves on the divider are used as a display area and there are also compartments designed to hold cutlery.

The worktops are tiled to offer a hard-wearing, practical and aesthetically pleasing surface. The white ceramic tiles continue up the wall to provide an easy-to-clean splashback area around the sink. A white and terracotta border has been incorporated to add pattern to the walls and to draw the floor colours up and around the window. The border has been finished off with narrow wooden beading, creating a neat edge to the tiles. There are a number of solutions to finishing a ceramic clad wall, includ-

ing the beading used here, or plastic trims which sit behind the tile and create a rounded edge. Alternatively, look for traditional rounded tiles, available in some ceramic ranges.

Casual elegance for
a family kitchen diner

The priority in this beautiful room is undoubtedly comfort and not the need for a large cooking and preparation area. However, you can still achieve a great deal in a small but well-planned kitchen. The room is split into different working areas which aesthetically combine to produce one large, pleasing room. The arched stone recess houses the cooker, low-level storage units and some discreet shelves on each side of the worktop, creating a compact space for preparation. The more traditional approach to an area like this one would have been to install a large range-type cooker, as may have originally been placed there. But in a room where space is at a premium it is better to include sensible storage.

Central to this arrangement is the oak table, providing a pleasant dining space as well as an extra work surface. To its right are the sink, dishwasher and refrigerator which have all been housed discreetly in buttermilk-painted units. These are the same colour as the walls to ensure the kitchen is as unobtrusive as possible, once again enhancing the feeling that the room is primarily one in which to relax.

The wonderful timber floor and stone-clad arch decorated with a pair of antlers add a country feel to the room so that it is somewhat reminiscent of a traditional hunting lodge. But the approach to the rest of the decor is less rustic. A break-front glazed cabinet houses a collection of traditional china and glass, to the side of which nestles a

DECORATIVE MOULDINGS
▼ Architectural devices such as mouldings, architraves and cornices were pivotal design elements of the townhouse room. They are available in a variety of patterns and can be painted or stained as you wish.

comfortable feather-filled sofa. The sofa sports blue scatter cushions and there is blue china on the coffee table. These are interesting additions as blue is a colour not used elsewhere in the room; instead, the majority of the scheme is made up of sunny creams and green. But the blue acts to add both a contrast of colour and to create a more informal edge to the room.

Finally, the room is completed with a well-chosen range of accessories. Note the informal collection of cards positioned on the wall above the sink. Each one is framed using a simple glass clip frame, which creates a cost-effective and casual display.

COMPACT KITCHEN

▲ The cooking area of the kitchen is truly compact. Bulky saucepans, colanders and sieves are left to hang rather than fill the small cupboards, and shelves are tucked into the recesses behind the stone arch.

Old-fashioned virtues combir
with modern practicality

**DETAILS,
DETAILS**

▼ Yellow and blue complement each other so beautifully that in a kitchen that features mellow timber and wicker baskets, blue paintwork and furnishings provide the perfect backdrop.

This beautiful painted kitchen looks as though it has evolved lovingly over a period of years. Instead, it is an excellent example of a contemporary painted kitchen which incorporates both traditional and modern features. For example, the square panelling and inset drawer fronts – teamed with details like the plate rack and free-standing dresser – are in the traditional mode. However, there are also elements of the built-in kitchen (the run of worktops, the cooker hood) that, together with contemporary paint techniques and colours, create an overall effect that is far from rustic.

Generally, the room has the feel of a totally free-standing kitchen, even though the majority of the units are fitted. This is achieved by keeping the run of worktops and base units to a minimum. Breaks in continuity, however small, create groups of units that act like selected individual pieces. For example, the housing for the extractor fan is attached to two small side units, whereas the plate rack is separated from its adjacent unit. Varying surface levels has the same effect, and adds extra interest to the layout. The ceramic tiles, too, are kept to a block around the cooking area, as opposed to running along the length of the worktops, as is more usual.

When you look at the pieces in detail, both the dresser and the main working area include identical design details – even the same handles. But by changing the colour of the units,

the effect is that of individual pieces of furniture, with different characters. This helps the kitchen to appear as if it has developed gradually rather than been clinically manufactured. The dresser does not look isolated, however, as the blue colour is cleverly echoed in the cupboard linings on the open units and also features in the ceramic tiles.

A quick and simple way to alter the feel of a kitchen is by changing the drawer and door knobs. These usually screw in and out very easily. Imagine how this kitchen would look if the knobs were much larger, or were made of brass or ceramic.

COMPLETING THE LOOK
▲ The room has a calm, slightly mellow feel due to the chosen flooring: stone, featuring flashes of warm peach and charcoal colours.

Soft milky creams
brightened with

This town house kitchen/dining room offers the best of smart family living. The functional kitchen is divided into two areas: the main food preparation area, which is accessed via the white panelled double doors, and the cooking and dining space in the well-proportioned main room. This is an interesting division as the cooking space would normally be positioned in the main preparation area, but informal dining can leave the chef in front of the stove while guests or family gather by the table. So why not place them together? This layout also means that any mess created when preparing the meal can still be well hidden behind the double doors.

The design of the units in the main room most definitely takes advantage of the high ceilings and the striking proportions. The stove is housed within a classical-style layout with a tiled back panel and recessed panelled door units, which offer ample storage. This is finished with routed columns and a classical pediment at the top. The columns stand proud of the base and outer side units, creating an interesting break at the front of what would otherwise have been a plain bank of fittings.

The double oven is housed in the side units to the left of the hob. This is counter-balanced by the tall unit with the same proportions on the opposite side – a layout that is fundamental to the overall appearance of the kitchen.

In essence, this kitchen has a very formal air, but the natural timber floor and plain timber table add

PLAIDS PROVIDE FLAIR

▼ Bright, modern plaids and large checks add flair to an otherwise plain or neutral room. Ivory, cream and natural terracotta provide the perfect foil for these strong but harmonious colours.

modern plaid

a more approachable feel. When this is teamed with the ample storage offered by this kitchen it creates a welcoming environment for a family, with plenty of room for the hustle and bustle of normal family life. At the same time, it is perfectly styled for a touch of town living.

STRIKING ARCHITECTURE
▼ Strong architectural details are enhanced in this town house kitchen diner. By keeping the colours muted, soft furnishings can afford to be bold.

FOCUS *file*

You will now be very familiar with the various styles of kitchen that are available, and if you are planning to replace or upgrade your own kitchen you have hopefully come a long way towards

making a decision about the style you would like in your home. The rooms featured in the Style File chapter on pages 10-59 will have given you a wide range of ideas and you will be able to determine why these rooms work so successfully, but there is still a large amount of information to help you make wise choices when selecting the principal elements that will make up your dream kitchen.

Over the next few pages, we examine the various peripheral products on the market from which you can make these all-important choices.

Sinks and worktops take a great deal of wear and tear in the domestic kitchen, so some background information of what is available will help you make the right decision. Technology has played a large role in developing materials that are ideal for the kitchen environment, having the beauty of traditional materials but the durability only space-age science can produce. We also look at the types of flooring and wallcoverings that are most suitable for a kitchen – those that withstand stains, steam, condensation and grease – together with information on lighting and window treatments.

It is a good idea to read all the sections within Focus File, especially if you are still unsure about the final look you want to achieve. There may be one item that really catches your imagination – a stone sink, or a tiled worksurface – or you may discover that a specific type of product may be more practical in your situation, making a decision easier to reach. Don't feel daunted, just enjoy the pleasure of making those decisions.

SHOP AROUND
▼ The choice is astonishing, so shop around, mix and match, and plan carefully to get the best kitchen for you.

Walls *and* floors

Wall and floor finishes need especially careful consideration in the kitchen as it is the one room in the home that is subjected to hard wear, vigorous cleaning and constant variations in temperature and humidity. This means that a fine balance must be met when choosing these finishes, weighing up practical considerations with aesthetic preferences.

If you are thinking of using wallpapers, then solid vinyl is an excellent option as it has a thick polymer coating which acts as a barrier to water penetration. Wallpapers are best avoided in areas subjected to constant steam or cleaning, however, as the colour and coating will eventually wear away, so areas such as behind the cooker and sink are best clad in a more robust product like paint, plastic or tiles.

Paints are a good option for the kitchen, and manufacturers now produce mildew and damp-resistant products especially for the kitchen and bathroom. Paints with an eggshell or vinyl finish are perfect, but if you like the sheen of high gloss, make sure you have adequate ventilation, as this can worsen condensation problems.

Graining, colourwashing, distressing and stencilling are now all part of the home decorator's list of achievable finishes. A great number of magazines and books are available that explain exactly how to re-create these effects if you are unsure.

It is also becoming increasingly popular to use

CLEAR LIGHT
▼ The glass blocks used in this kitchen act as both a construction material and a decorative finish, giving the room light and vitality.

RUSTIC TILES
◀ ▼ Hand-decorated ceramic and terracotta tiles from all parts of the world are now readily available to the home decorator. They add an individual touch that cannot be emulated by any other product.

water-based paints on all surfaces in the kitchen to make colour matching easier. In such cases, protect the woodwork with a coat or two of acrylic varnish. This is worthwhile on a distressed paint finish on, say, furniture or skirting boards.

Many colour schemes include stained and painted timber – either natural tones or more colourful washes – for both walls and floors. And with a quality varnish and sealant over the top, most timbers can now be used in areas such as the sink without danger of warping or distortion.

Ceramic, marble and quarry tiles offer a very versatile and practical finish for both walls and floors in a kitchen. These natural products will withstand a great deal of wear and are available in practically every colour, pattern and style imaginable.

PAINTERLY DETAILS

◄ Here, paint finishes have been used to decorate both walls and floor. The timber floor has been painted and stencilled, while a more fanciful stencil has been applied to the plain white walls. A metallic paint effect gives the splashbacks and kitchen units added interest.

Ceramic tiles are particularly varied and can be laid in patterns of your own choice. Consider combining different colours of the same hand-painted motif, using moulded dado rails, or insetting picture tiles among plain white tiles. If you are planning on using tiles as a splashback, take advantage of the modern adhesives and grouts now available as they team with the product to create a bacteria-free and hard-wearing surface.

For the floor, in addition to ceramic tiles, there is also a wonderful selection of slate, terracotta and stone, all of which are extremely hard-wearing. These products have a unique quality and style, but will need more maintenance than other types of hard flooring if they are to avoid greasy stains becoming permanent. They are also expensive options, will definitely need laying by an expert, are hard underfoot, and any dropped dishes will undoubtedly break on such a surface, so bear these points in mind when making your choice.

Softer floorings include natural timber, cork tiles and vinyl which together offer an extensive palette of colours and designs for your kitchen. If you are laying cork or vinyl, it is best to prepare the bare floor first by laying small sheets of hardboard. Soak the boards first and lay them rough side up, securing them with ring nails. These have more grip than ordinary nails and will prevent the floor surface from shifting later on.

Cushion vinyl is a cheaper and warmer alternative to hard tiles and there are many very passable imitations available both as tiles and sheet flooring. The disadvantage of using timber or vinyl is the fact that water can penetrate to the floor below. So if any of your appliances were to overflow or leak, you could end up with problems. You should therefore choose these types of product with care.

FINISHING TOUCHES
▲ Ceramic tiles now incorporate every style and theme of decorating imaginable. This little badger would bring a smile to your face on the busiest of days.

HARD WEARING
▼ Small insets between larger floor tiles break up a surface and give it added interest.

Work surfaces *and* sinks

Two of the main areas in your kitchen that will take most of the wear and tear are the sink and worktop areas. There is now an extremely large choice of products available to fulfil both the practical requirements within a busy kitchen and your aesthetic needs, to enhance your chosen style of decor.

In the traditional kitchen, natural finishes and products with conventional origins obviously work best. Wooden worktops can be used throughout or can be used alongside ceramic tiled surfaces in country or traditional styles. But choose wooden work tops with care as not all timber is suitable – hardwood is best – and all will require a certain amount of maintenance in the form of oiling or waxing to keep the wood waterproof and looking its best.

VERSATILE TILES

▼ Don't restrict ceramic tiles to walls and floors – they make perfect worksurfaces, providing you choose ones specifically designed for the purpose.

Ceramic tiles come in a very wide range of styles and designs and they look at home in all settings, not just the traditional interior. Sadly, many people have been put off using ceramics for worktops because of problems encountered in the past. For example, thin 'biscuit' wall tiles are not substantial enough to withstand the possible impact from heavy pots and pans and any worksurface fitted with these will have witnessed some disastrous results. Fortunately, there are now suitable tiles that can be used, but make sure that you choose a tile with a glaze that will not discolour. Likewise, grout used to be rather unstable, but all this is in the past now. Modern technology has supplied us with epoxy adhesives and grouts which when used correctly create a surface that is impervious to germs and dirt.

Granite is another increasingly popular alternative for work surfaces, offering a variety of colour choices. Granite can make a very serviceable worktop, as it is both hard wearing and easy to clean. If you choose to use either granite or marble, it should be cut and installed by an expert and allowances made for a variation of colour between each sheet – after all, this is a natural product.

Modern products, such as laminates and Corian, in finishes that emulate the above products, also have their place in the traditional kitchen. These can have the same overall effect on the design of your room as the original, with the added benefit of

TWO-TONE
◄ The modern sink is available in almost any colour and style imaginable. Here, the two-tone colourway adds an interesting feature.

TONING-IN
▲ A laminated worktop with a timber edge that matches the rest of the kitchen acts as a housing for a small, well-designed white enamelled sink.

PRACTICAL FEATURES

▲ A modern sink unit with a deep bowl and high rim prevents water from splashing onto the neighbouring worktop. The sliding cutting board is a useful feature.

SHINING SURFACES

▼ As people take home entertaining and food preparation more seriously, products traditionally used in the professional kitchen are now being used in a domestic setting.

the advantages that come from modern technology. In many cases, these products can, in fact, be more cost effective that the natural finishes that are available.

When deciding on contemporary worktops for the kitchen, you are spoilt for choice as manufacturers now produce every shade and finish of laminate imaginable. In addition, products like Corian can be cast in any colour and shape to form worktops that incorporate sink and drainer areas. These finishes also have the benefit of being non-porous, and as they are solid, can be sanded and polished to remove any blemishes and burns that may occur over time.

Used less now for worktops are thin laminate veneers, which are bonded to a base of either chipboard, ply-board or MDF. These finishes are serviceable and easy to clean, but they should not be used as a cutting or chopping surface as a knife will penetrate the surface, creating a weak spot through which moisture can penetrate, possibly causing the timber below to swell and distort.

Chrome, a product traditionally associated with the professional kitchen and once reserved just for the sink, has now become widely used in the domestic setting as a hard-wearing worktop, splash back, cooker hood or storage.

Clay and stone sinks look wonderful in a truly traditional setting, but are quite difficult to obtain. A good alternative is the practical Belfast – or butler's – sink which has grown in popularity recently and is also easily available, offering a

OLD STYLE
◄ This old stone sink and wall-mounted taps look wonderful in a traditional setting, but they can be hard to obtain. If you have your heart set on one, contact your local stone mason to see if a sink can be made specially for you.

substantial washing facility for the traditional kitchen. There is also a number of companies specializing in ceramic, brass and enamelware, all of which can create an eye-catching feature within the kitchen.

Kitchen and appliance designers are now spending as much time on the design and development of the domestic sink and drainer as they do a piece of art. Finally, keep in mind the functions of your sink area, as you are no longer restricted to a bowl and draining board. Look out for single and double drainers, half and single bowls, integrated chopping boards, inset draining racks, waste disposal units – the selection is enormous.

Storage *ideas*

ALL STORED AWAY

▼ Cupboards and drawers come in a wide variety of shapes and sizes which is just what is needed to make the most of storing the contents of a kitchen.

Many people make the mistake of thinking that the more cup-boards you have in the kitchen, the better. While it may be true to say that you can never have too many well-designed storage units, efficient organization of the contents of your kitchen offers a better solution. Cupboards need not only be at ground level, nor need they all be of the same height. Units attached to walls at eye-level height make good use of what can often be wasted space. They are also especially useful for storing items that need to be kept away from children's sticky fingers or, if you have glass-fronted doors, for displaying favourite pieces of china or dinnerware. If there is space, a large cupboard that reaches

to the ceiling will provide splendid opportunities for storage.

Open plate racks or shelves are the perfect home for everyday china, and again add decorative detail to the room while supplying storage that is easily accessible. Position such storage racks within easy reach of the dishwasher or sink to save time and breakages.

For those who have moved into an older house in which there is a pantry, please think twice before having it removed. Unless the kitchen is extremely small, the traditional shelved, walk-in pantry can house far more than the best fitted kitchen layout. Originally, the pantry would have been situated on an outside wall with good ventilation and this – coupled with a stone floor – would have created a cool, airy space. Today, despite central heating, pantries are still surprisingly efficient at keeping food and wine cool. In fact, many kitchen designers are now incorporating large floor to ceiling pantry or larder cupboards to replace the originals.

Modern designs of kitchen offer many storage solutions, such as fold-away ironing boards, pull-out rubbish bins and tables, and waste disposal units to keep the kitchen as streamlined as possible. Drawers of varying sizes are especially useful for storing different sized items. Small drawers are great for cutlery and tea-towels, say, while deep drawers make it easy to store larger items like casserole dishes and stacks of plates. Plan your requirements and then choose your units accordingly.

HANG-UPS
◀ Saucepans and other kitchen utensils can be decorative so hang them up as a display and use the cupboards for other, less attractive, kitchenware.

SMALL SPACES
▼ If you have room to stow a large refrigerator elsewhere, you will find it useful to keep a small one in the kitchen for everyday items.

NOVEL STORES
▲ A mixture of storage in a contemporary, Shaker style. The peg board is set around the whole room and is perfect for hanging almost anything; the wicker drawers not only look good but also provide excellent storage for fruit and vegetables. And note the useful and decorative plate rack.

WASTED SPACE
▶ These attractive wall units, designed in Art Deco style, provide storage with flair. Remember that wall units make good use of areas that would otherwise be wasted.

Unless totally bespoke, even the modern fitted kitchen will have the odd space where the smallest standard unit is too large to fit. Ask a carpenter to help you adapt these spaces to house thin baking tins or chopping boards, and consider replacing the plinth panels at the bottom of your kitchen base units with custom-made drawers to store linen or baking equipment. All too often it is these last pieces of equipment with their awkward shapes that clutter full-size cupboards.

If you have the advantage of a separate utility room, use it to house a large refrigerator or freezer, and fit a small integrated larder refrigerator, which will take up minimum space, in the kitchen. This can house the items that you most regularly use such as milk, butter and cheese, while larger items can be stored elsewhere until needed.

Be ruthless when it comes to organizing the contents of your kitchen. If something is used less than once a week it should not

take up prime-access storage space. Conversely, condiments, herbs, spices and oils used regularly in cooking should be kept near to the cooker and easily accessible. Cooking pots and pans should be within easy reach, too, and can even add atmosphere to a room if displayed within view. This then frees up valuable cupboard space for other, less attractive, items, or items that are used less frequently.

The kitchen with good storage, then, has a mixture of built-in and open storage that has been carefully planned. This, combined with the good positioning of the contents of your kitchen, will offer you the best in storage solutions.

MAKING THE MOST OF IT
▲ A well-planned kitchen has plenty of storage space. Mix glass-fronted cupboards with those that conceal appliances and unattractive cookware.

Window *treatments*

Unless your kitchen is very grand or incorporates a formal dining area, the secret to successful kitchen window treatments lies in simplicity. Because kitchen curtains need more regular laundering than those in any other room in the home they should be simple to remove, re-attach and dress, and preferably be made from easily washable fabrics. Be aware, however, that most lined curtains should, where possible, be dry cleaned as even if the main fabric is washable, the linings may shrink.

Roman blinds are one simple option in a kitchen. There is very little fabric to trap dust and grime and they can be made in almost any fabric, and create an impact on the design of a room.

SIMPLE TIES
▼ Simple, unlined curtains such as these can be quickly removed and laundered – a necessity in a steamy kitchen. Ties in a contrast fabric, rather than more formal hooks, are used to hang the curtains on the pole.

DRAPING FABRIC

◀ If your kitchen has a private outlook you may decide not to use a curtain or blind and opt for a simple drape of fabric that frames the window instead. To achieve this effect, buy metal 'spiral' holders which enable you to wind the fabric into attractive knots at each top corner.

They are also very simple to operate and are easily drawn up when not in use, making them less likely to get in the way of wall-mounted units or sink and cooker areas.

If you are the sort of person who tires of things easily, then a drape made of a simple square of fabric the size of your window recess will offer you the option of change. As you can see here, the same square has been attached to a window frame using ornate metal hooks, and it can be drawn up into a blind with two simple ties. The same drape can also be drawn to one side of the window to create a curtain using a tie.

Of course, fabric window treatments are not the only option. Wooden shutters and various forms of blind are also available – everything from the metal or timber Venetian blind to the simple rafia roller. Stained glass or shelves set into the window recess are alternative ways of creating privacy in a decorative manner without the use of traditional curtains and blinds.

CHECKS AND SQUARES

▼ This square of fabric is made of an unlined, large check cotton fabric, which has been framed with a border of the same fabric cut on the cross. It can easily be draw in to one side of the window and fastened with a tie.

Lighting

NIGHT LIGHTS
▲ Little can beat natural light, but at night discreet recessed halogen spots assisted by concealed under-cupboard lighting come into their own.

While most designers spend a great deal of time considering the correct combination of lighting for each room in the home, I suspect that the kitchen is the one room where most people would instinctively consider mixing different types of lighting. Common sense dictates that a kitchen should never be lit solely by a single central light as it will cast a shadow onto working areas and will not provide sufficient illumination. Many kitchens have a combination of central and under-unit concealed lighting, which is usually quite sufficient.

Fluorescent lighting has been used in domestic kitchens for many years. It is energy-efficient and gives out very little heat. However, the strips can sometimes emit a buzz and the light produced is very harsh and must be covered by a shade or shielded from the eye – it can cause damage if you look directly into its light. Fluorescent bulbs are also expensive to dim as they require additional connections to achieve this.

Halogen lighting has become very popular in recent years. It takes it name from the fact that it is filled with halogen gas, enabling the bulb to reach very high temperatures which creates a very white light. This is part of the attraction as halogen lights produce true colours which do not distort.

Halogen spot- and recess lights are very small and unobtrusive, ideal for use with other forms of lighting. The bulbs are available in various strengths and widths of beam. This means you can use one bulb to create a wash of light while another can add a direct shaft of light using a narrow width of beam. How-

ever, take care when positioning halogen lights close to soft furnishings as they could be a fire hazard.

Tungsten has a shorter life expectancy than either fluorescent or halogen bulbs; it doesn't emit too much heat and is easily dimmed. However, tungsten bulbs produce a mellow, slightly yellow light, which is more true than fluorescent but it does sometimes affect the colour of furnishings in the absence of natural light.

Install light switches at elbow height so they can easily be flicked on or off if your hands are full. Two-way switches are also essential if you have both an outside and inside door.

CONCEALED STRIPS

▲ The interesting shafts of light reflected in the metal splash backs are produced by short lengths of concealed strip lighting.

SNAKING LIGHTS

◄ This contemporary kitchen is enhanced by modern halogen light fittings, which offer peaks of directional lighting.

Stockists and contributors

Alno UK
Unit 10
Hampton Farm Industrial Estate
Hampton Road West
Hanworth
Middlesex TW13 6DB
Tel: 0181 898 4781
Fax: 0181 898 0268
(Kitchen furniture)

Andrew Macintosh Furniture
462/464 Chiswick High Road
London W4 5TT
Tel: 0181 995 8333
Fax: 0181 995 8999

Artisan
4a Union Court
20 Union Road
London SW4 6JP
Tel: 0171 498 6974
(Contemporary and classic
curtain rails)

Atag (UK)
19 Hither Green
Clevedon
Avon BS21 6XU
Tel: 01275 877301
Fax: 01275 871371
(Built-in kitchen appliances)

Blanco
Oxgate Lane
Cricklewood
London NW2 7JN
Tel: 0181 450 9100
Fax: 0800 282 846
(Sinks and taps)

Chalon
Hambridge Mill
Hambridge
Somerset TA10 0BP
Tel: 01458 252374
Fax: 01458 251192
(Formal country furniture)

Colorol
Riverside Mills
Crawford Street
Nelson
Lancashire B9 7QT
Tel: 01282 617777
(Fabrics and wallpapers)

Crown Paints
Tel: 01254 704951
(For stockists)

Divertimenti
P.O. Box 6611
London SW6 6XU
(Kitchen equipment)

Dulux Paints
Tel: 01753 550555

Fired Earth
Twyford Mill
Oxford Road
Adderbury
Oxfordshire OX17 3HP
Tel: 01295 812088
Fax: 01295 810832
(Tiles, flooring, fabrics)

Forbes & Lomax Ltd
205b St John's Hill
London SW11 1TH
Tel: 0171 738 0202
(Contemporary light
switches and accessories)

Forbo-Nairn
PO Box 1
Kircaldy
Fife KY1 2SB
Tel: 01592 643111
Fax: 01592 643999
(Linoleum and vinyl flooring)

Franke UK
East Park
Manchester International Office
Centre
Styal Road
Manchester M22 5WB
(Sinks, taps and eco-recycling
systems)

Habitat
Head Office
Tel: 0171 255 2545

The Holding Company Ltd
Unit 15, Imperial Studio
3-11 Imperial Road
London SW6 2AG
Tel: 0171 610 9160
Fax: 0171 610 9166
(Mail order with one outlet in the
King's Road, London)

Intoto Kitchens
Wakefield Road
Leeds
West Yorkshire LS27 7JZ
Tel: 0113 252 4131
Fax: 0113 252 0154

Laura Ashley
Customer services
PO Box 19
Newtown
Powys SY16 1DZ
Tel: 01686 622116

Mark Wilkinson
Overton House
High Street
Bromham
Chippenham SN15 2HA
Tel: 01380 850004
Fax: 01380 850184
(Kitchen furniture)

Merloni Domestic Appliances
Merloni House
3 Cowley Business Park
Cowley
Uxbridge
Middlesex UB8 2AD
Tel: 01895 858200
Fax: 01895 858269
(New World cookers)

MFI
For details of your nearest
store phone
Freepages 0500 192 192

Mr Light
279 Kings Road
London SW3 5EW
Tel: 0171 401 2310
(Contemporary lighting)

Shaker
25 Harcourt Street
London W1H 1DT
Tel: 0171 724 7672
Fax: 0171 724 6640
and
322 Kings Road
London SW3 5UH
(Furniture, gifts and
accessories. Mail order
available)

Smallbone of Devizes
105–109 Fulham Road
London SW3
Tel: 0171 581 9989
(Kitchen Furniture)

Smeg (UK)
Corinthian Court
80 Milton Park
Abingdon
Oxon OX14 4RY
Tel: 01235 861090
Fax: 01235 861120
(Hobs, ovens and hoods)

Specialist Crafts Ltd
PO Box 247
Leicester LE1 9QS
Tel: 0116 251 0405
Fax: 0116 251 5015
(Mail order - large supply of
craft materials)

Stanley Cookers
Abbey Road
Wrexham Industrial Estate
Wrexham LL13 9RF
Tel: 01978 664555
Fax: 01978 664567
(Cast iron cookers)

The Stencil Store Group
Head Office
20/21 Heronsgate Road
Chorleywood
Herts WD3 5BN
Tel: 01923 285577/88
Fax: 01923 285136

Stoves
Stoney Lane
Prescot
Merseyside L35 2XW
Tel: 0151 426 6551
Fax: 0151 426 3261

William Ball
Gumley Road
Grays
Essex RM20 4WB
Tel: 01375 375151
(Built-in kitchens)

SOUTH AFRICA

The Building Centre
209 Cartwrights Corner House
Adderley Street
Cape Town 8001
Western Cape
Tel: (021) 86-7070
Fax: (021) 86-6348

Buildex
PO Box 1616
Bedfordview 2008
Bauteng
Tel: (011) 455-6002
Fax: (011) 455-6013

The Natal Master Builders Exhibition Centre
40 Essex Terrace
Westville 3630
KwaZulu-Natal
Tel: (031) 86-7070
Fax: (031) 86-6348

AUSTRALIA

BBC Hardware
(branches throughout Australia)
Building A, Cnr Cambridge &
Chester Street
Epping NSW 2121
Tel: 02 9876 0888

Home Hardware
(branches throughout NSW)
15 Huntingwood Drive
Huntingwood NSW 2148
Tel: 02 9839 0777

Mitre 10
(branches throughout VIC)
12 Dansu Court Hallam
Princes Highway VIC 3803
Tel: 03 9796 4999

True Value Hardware
(branches throughout SA)
1367 Main North Road
Para West Hills SA 5096
Tel: 08 8281 2244
(branches throughout Qld)
16 Cambridge Street
Rocklea Qld 4106
Tel: 08 3892 0892

Makit Hardware
(branches throughout WA)
87 President Street
Welshpool WA 3966
Tel: 08 9351 8001

NEW ZEALAND

Jacobsen Ceramic Tiles & Wood Flooring
228 Orakei Road
Remuera
Auckland
Tel: (09) 524 1460

Auckland Sink Top Fabricators Ltd
19D Cartwright Road
Glen Eden
Tel: (09) 818 4746

Kitchen Trends Ltd
86B Wairau Road
Glenfield
Tel: (09) 444 4324

Kitchens & Appliances
220 Station Road
Penrose
Tel: (09) 525 1001

Plumbing World
76-78 Ellice Road
Glenfield
Tel: (09) 444 6452

ACKNOWLEDGEMENTS

The author and publishers would like to thank the following companies and their PR agencies for their kind assistance in the loan of photographs and props used in this book. We have taken care to ensure that we have acknowledged everyone and we apologise if, in error, we have omitted anyone.

For their kind loan of props:
Chloe Gardner, tile, page 16; Charles Harden, door knobs, page 20; Delaine Le Bas, blind, page 30; Jenny King, flower swag, page 39; Moira Neal, Lynda Howarth, painted glass, page 53; Heather Luke, blind, page 75.

For use of transparencies:
Alno Kitchens: page 11br, 33, 47b; Andrew Macintosh Furniture: pages 9b; 22b, 70, 71t; Atag: page 6t, 9t; Bisque radiators: page 25b; Blanco UK: 68t; Fired Earth: page 63b, 65t and b; Formica: page 67t; Hickman & Associates: page 11bl; Mark Wilkinson kitchens: pages 20–21; MFI: pages 38, 49t and b, 73; Nolte Kitchens: pages 25t, 61, 72; PJ Leiderer Industrie: page 67b; Smallbone of Devizes: pages 19, 41b, 57; Stanley Cookers: pages 45t; Wellmann Contessa: pages 13b, 22t; William Ball: page 8

Picture Credits:

Abode: title page, pages 7, 10, 29, 35b, 37t, 51b, 64, 66, 72t, 74, 75t
C. Simon Sykes/The Interior Archive: pages 42, 44
Elizabeth Whiting Associates: pages 17, 35t, 52, 59;
Henry Wilson/The Interior Archive: pages 12, 23b, 43b, 62
J. Pilkington/The Interior Archive: pages 15, 43t
Ray Main/Mainstream Photography: cover, pages 5, 11tl and r, 76, 77b
Schulenburg/The Interior Archive: pages 13t, 24, 31, 50, 51t, 63t, 69, 77t
Simon Brown/The Interior Archive: pages 6b, 26, 68b
Simon Upton/The Interior Archive: page 55
Tim Beddow/The Interior Archive: page 23t, 34

Index